SQUANTO
AND THE FIRST THANKSGIVING

SQUANTO
AND THE FIRST THANKSGIVING

written by Eric Metaxas • illustrated by Michael A. Donato

Rabbit Ears Books

Editor's Note: The audiocassette accompanying this book is a theatrical rendition and does
not exactly match the text in the book.

Rabbit Ears Books is an imprint of Rabbit Ears Productions, Inc.
Published by Simon & Schuster, Inc.
1230 Avenue of the Americas
New York, New York 10020

Library of Congress Cataloging-in-Publication Data

Metaxas, Eric
Squanto and the first Thanksgiving / written by Eric Metaxas :
illustrated by Michael A. Donato.
p.   cm.
Summary: A biography of the Pawtuxet Indian who, after his capture, escape, and return
to his childhood home, helped the Pilgrims establish the colony of Plymouth.
ISBN 0-689-80234-X
1. Squanto—Juvenile literature. 2. Wampanoag Indians—Biography—Juvenile literature.
3. Pilgrims (New Plymouth Colony)—Juvenile literature. 4. Thanksgiving Day—Juvenile
literature. [1. Squanto. 2. Wampanoag Indians—Biography. 3. Indians of North
America—Biography. 4. Pilgrims (New Plymouth Colony) 5. Thanksgiving Day.]
I. Donato, Michael A., ill. II. Title.
E99.W2S644   1996
973.2'1—dc20   95-36723   CIP   AC

For Alexander Perretti, with love—E. M.

For Theresa, Michael-Vincent, and Dad—M. D.

Long, long ago, when the white man's visits to the New World were as infrequent as comets and eclipses, there lived in the land that is now called Massachusetts a proud and noble people called the Pawtuxets.

The Pawtuxets lived on a gentle rise of land overlooking the ocean, in round wigwams made of bent saplings and tree bark, in a village surrounded by great golden fields of corn that swayed in the breezes that rose up from the bluefish-colored sea.

And when the corn of many colors ripened in its ear, drawing the hungry crows, it was the job of the children of the village to chase them away. One could hear their young voices mingling with the jaded *caw-caw* of the crows in the field.

One of these voices belonged to a boy named Tisquantum. Tisquantum, or Squanto as he was called, was zealous in frightening away the shiny blackbirds, for he had been among those who had planted the corn in the spring so many months before, when the dogwoods were beginning to bud pink and white, and the mountains were a chilly wash of early greens and innocent reds, and the laughing streams were filled with the fish called alewives.

It was the custom of the Pawtuxets during planting season to put two or three of these fish in each hole with the corn to make the soil rich. Then beans were planted next to the corn and, when the beanstalks grew, they climbed up the strong cornstalks.

Squanto also helped plant pumpkins and gourds and squash. He helped gather wild strawberries in the woods and blackberries and cranberries, which his mother and the other women cooked in pies. Sometimes he went in the woods with his father to check the twine snares they had set to catch wild turkeys.

When Squanto was a little older he fished in the ocean, catching cod and bass and other large fish. And when he was almost a man, Squanto went with his father and the elders of the tribe in canoes to hunt the great whales that lived in the deep waters of the endless shifting ocean.

While he was out on the quiet water, so far from land, Squanto remembered the stories he had heard of those foreign people who lived beyond the ocean in the place where the orange sun rose. It was said that in the time of his great-great-grandfather, they had come across the curved water in towering canoes to trade tools and pots and other things for the rich pelts of beaver. They were said to have white skin and hair growing on their faces. *What were they like?* he wondered. *Were they cruel or kind?*

Then one day, some years later, after Squanto had left the world of childhood and had become a man, he saw something far out on the water. What he saw was even larger than one of the great whales themselves. It was one of the canoes of the white men.

When some of these foreign visitors came ashore to build a fire, Squanto and some of the other men went to watch them from the woods. He marveled at their odd clothing and at their white skin and hair-covered jaws. They were just as he had been told. And they spoke a queer, unintelligible tongue. But they didn't appear to have anything to trade. At last Squanto decided to meet them.

The men seemed friendly, but their leader was less so. His name was Captain Hunt, and there was something about him that Squanto did not trust. He made motions that they should come to the ship to trade. But when Squanto resisted the idea, Captain Hunt and the others revealed their true colors: They overcame Squanto and the three other men, brutally knocking them to the ground and tying their hands and feet. In moments, Squanto and the other men were taken to the ship and thrown into the hold below the deck.

When at last Squanto awoke, his head ached terribly. The ship's hold was cramped and dark, but he could feel the great boat moving over the water. He and his three companions weren't the only prisoners. There must have been twenty men in there with him.

Time passed, days and nights. The conversation was sparse. Squanto's mind wandered back to his childhood. And he remembered the faces of those who had died many winters ago.

Perhaps I too have died, Squanto thought, *and perhaps I am now making the journey of the dead. And perhaps I will be reborn into the land of the spirits on the other side of the world, in the land of light, where the sun god dwells.*

After many days of suffering, Squanto was summoned above deck by one of the sailors. At first the harsh light blinded him, and for some moments he thought perhaps he had at last arrived on the other side of the world. But when his eyes became used to his surroundings, Squanto saw that he was only on a wooden vessel among men.

Sometimes the sailors communicated with them, but Captain Hunt did not so much as look any of his captives in the eye. When they finally spied land, Squanto learned that he was going to be sold.

The port they landed in was a city called Málaga, in the country of

Spain. The people who had come to buy slaves were even worse than the sailors on the ship. But there were on the edge of all this commotion some men who did not look like the others. They wore long robes of brown cloth and had no hair on the tops of their heads. One of them approached Hunt, and it was decided that Squanto would go with them.

Squanto lived among these men, called friars, for some time. They nursed him back to health, and afterward, although he worked for them in the fields, he was not treated as a slave. Squanto marveled at the warmth of the land and at the tame animals they called horses and at the cows and sheep that gave them milk and cheese. But even though Squanto grew fond of these men and of the sun-baked land in which they lived, he longed to return to his home and to his people.

After two years the friars arranged for Squanto to go to London. There he would work for a man named John Slany who was a merchant who sometimes sent ships to Newfoundland in North America. Perhaps he would be able to offer Squanto passage back home.

When Squanto arrived in London, he couldn't believe his eyes. He had never seen so many people. Squanto stayed with John Slany as a stable hand, and he learned the ways of the English.

Slany knew how Squanto longed to return to his people, and he promised Squanto that someday soon a ship would bring him back. But that day never seemed to come. Then, after he had waited more than two full years, a ship was found that was going to the New World. At last Squanto was going home.

And so one bright day Squanto said good-bye to John Slany and boarded a ship at the London docks.

This ship carried him back across the great water, which the English called the Atlantic Ocean. They landed in Newfoundland, where Squanto met a man who was going to sail south along the coast toward the area near Pawtuxet. He would bring Squanto home.

Finally, after many weeks, they neared the coast of Squanto's beloved home. He was brought to the shore only a few miles from Pawtuxet. He bade the sailors good-bye and began walking, drinking in the familiar sights of his boyhood haunts. Squanto's heart leapt. Soon he would be home! As fast as his legs could carry him, he ran toward Pawtuxet.

Finally, his chest heaving, he arrived at the place where he had been a boy, chasing crows among the cornfields. But there was no one to greet him. Squanto stared at the empty clearing. Where there had been the merry sounds of children and dogs running about, there was silence; where there had been warmth from cooking fires, there was coldness. The cornfields lay fallow. Squanto longed desperately to see the fields of colored corn and to hear the sounds of life in Pawtuxet village again. *What had happened?*

And so Squanto went to live among the nearby Nemasket people. They told him that the Pawtuxets had been destroyed by a plague that the English called smallpox. Everyone had perished. They too had lost many to the deadly plague.

After all of his wandering, it had come to this.

Squanto was welcomed among the Nemaskets, but these people were not his people, and this village was not his home. Squanto's sadness grew.

After many months he left the Nemaskets and went to live alone in the woods nearby. Winter came and went.

Then one day in the spring, Squanto was visited by a man named Samoset. He told Squanto of strange new happenings in Pawtuxet. An entire ship of English people had come ashore and had even built

 wigwams there. Samoset had been to meet them, and he urged Squanto to return with him. At first Squanto resisted, but finally he decided to go, and what he saw there amazed him. There in Pawtuxet, where he had grown up, were dozens of people dressed precisely like the people in England.

"Good morning!" Squanto said. "It is a beautiful morning."

The English people were amazed to hear these words. They had traveled so far, and now, out of the wilds of their new home, came a native man speaking their own language. It was more than amazing!

Two of the English, one man named William Bradford and another named John Alden, told Squanto their story: how they had wandered from place to place wanting to worship God in their own way. Squanto had heard of these wandering people, called Pilgrims, when he lived in London, and how they had been cruelly persecuted by King James. And now Squanto was sitting with them in the very place where he had been a boy, in the same clearing, near the very same trees that he had climbed.

Pilgrims in Pawtuxet!

They told Squanto of their trip aboard the ship called the *Mayflower* and of their harrowing first winter in which so many had died. Some of them had come to know the fathomless sorrow of watching their entire families perish. Then Squanto told Bradford his tale of woe.

"We are brothers in sorrow," he told William Bradford, "you and I."

Squanto decided to remain among these people for a time. He showed them how to trap alewives in the streams as he had done as a boy, and he showed them how to put three of these fish in with each few kernels of corn to make them grow strong. He taught the children how to stomp the mud in the streambeds, so that fat eels would come squirming out, and  he taught them to make snares to catch wild turkeys. He showed them how to catch lobsters and where to dig for shellfish along the shore.

He helped them to negotiate a peace treaty with the great chief Massasoit. Suddenly, for the first time since they had arrived, it appeared that there was hope for this weary band of wanderers. Squanto's appearance among them had been a miracle.

At harvest time the elders of the Plymouth Plantation were so thankful for the bountiful provision that had been made for them that they decided to appoint a special feast to thank God for his blessings. And as a sign of goodwill they invited the great chief Massasoit and his warriors to join them.

On the appointed day, Massasoit arrived with a train of ninety of his best warriors. They brought gifts of five deer along with many wild turkeys and other foods. There was eel and cod and lobster and quahogs and mussels and wild turkey and cranberries and succotash and berry pies. The men taught the English children native games, and everyone laughed. The great feast of Thanksgiving continued for three full days.

Squanto ate great helpings of Pawtuxet corn. He watched the children playing and listened to the sea breezes move through the trees.

At last from great want and sorrow had bloomed abundance and joy: There was life in the Pawtuxet village again.

The noble Pawtuxet called
Squanto died in the English year
1622, only a year after this first
Thanksgiving, but those earnest
people whom his kind heart
touched would never forget him.